C000008529

Restored Lives

Recovery from divorce and separation

WORKBOOK
in conjunction with the Restored Lives course and DVD

Erik Castenskiold

MONARCH
BOOKS
Oxford, UK & Grand Rapids, Michigan, USA

Published by Monarch Books
an imprint of
Lion Hudson plc
Wilkinson House, Jordan Hill Road,
Oxford OX2 8DR, England
Email: monarch@lionhudson.com
www.lionhudson.com/monarch

ISBN 978 0 85721 478 2
ISBN 987 0 85721 477 5 (pack of five)

First edition 2013

A catalogue record for this book is available from the British Library

Printed and bound in the UK, September 2013, LH32

In the Restored Lives book and DVD a number of stories are told of
people who have attended the Restored Lives course. In relationship
breakdown there are often two different sides to the same story, and
someone else close to the situation may view things differently. As a
result, I have sought to be respectful of both parties and to present
the facts neutrally, while focusing on the journey of the storyteller. In
addition, all names and key identifying features have been changed to
preserve anonymity.

Contents

Session 1
Facing the effects of what's happened   4

Session 2
Communication and conflict resolution   9

Session 3
Letting go   15

Session 4
Managing other relationships   20

Session 5
Legal matters   27

Session 6
Being single and moving forward   34

Session 1

Facing the effects of what's happened

Welcome

It can take courage to come on the Restored Lives course – well done for making it here.

You will all be at slightly different stages, but the course is designed for everyone.

You may feel intensely lonely, but here on this course **you are not alone**.

Everyone on the team understands what it's like to go through divorce and separation.

The course is designed for anyone of any faith or background.

We will be looking at the building blocks for successful recovery, and each one of the sessions is important in the process of moving on.

Three common things about relationship breakdown:

1. Divorce and separation represent a loss and this hurts – it helps to acknowledge this.

2. Accepting that the events have occurred is a crucial first step in the recovery process.

3. There is hope – amidst the despair, there is a real hope of having a restored life in the future.

We **cannot** change the past or our ex, but we **can** change ourselves, and that will affect our future.

Small groups are an important part of the course, in which everyone can participate if they want to. Please keep discussions confidential.

Small-group exercise

Discuss within your group how you came to be on this course.

The pain of loss

Some people find that their divorce is relatively painless. Others find themselves consumed by the pain of the losses caused by separation and divorce.

We have lost our partner and, because of that, we have sustained a series of related losses.

We need to understand when and why we feel pain so that we can help relieve it and recover more quickly.

Why talk about these things if they are apparently well hidden? If we don't, the pain will act like a landmine inside us, ready to explode at any unexpected trigger.

We should not ignore the pain of these losses because **pain, physical or emotional,** demands **action**.

The recovery process

A diagram of the journey through divorce and separation:

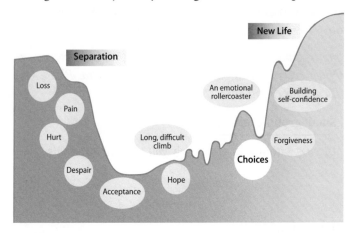

Time is not the healer, it's the choices we make that dictate the speed of our recovery.

We can move quickly from being a normal, interesting human being to a confused bag of emotions. This downward curve is temporary. The intensity of our emotions *will* change.

Group exercise

What emotions have you experienced in respect of your separation or divorce?

Personal story: How to deal with some of these thoughts and feelings.

Small-group exercise

What has helped you in dealing with these thoughts and feelings?

Holding on to hope

However hard things are, there *is* hope for us all.

We may have a failed relationship; but we are not failures.

You have other successful relationships, gifts, talents, and skills.

We have experienced a huge change and we need to adjust to a new set of circumstances.

Top ten suggestions to help deal with the pain on a daily basis:

1. Take one day at a time. *Notice the present.*

2. Start writing a journal.

3. Understand that you are grieving for the loss of your relationship.

4. Appreciate others.

5. Be kind to yourself. *Limit the things I find frustrating + difficult*

6. Count your blessings at the end of each day.

7. Enjoy laughter.

8. Take some physical exercise.

9. Help others.

10. Seek help where necessary.

Small-group exercise

What practical things do you find helpful for day-to-day survival? What would you like to get out of this course?

You will adjust to your new set of circumstances, and can learn from your experience of breakdown to make the future better.

This course is about restoring lives and giving you real hope for the future.

There *is* life after separation and divorce.

Session 2

Communication and conflict resolution

Small-group exercise

What did you find useful/helpful from the last session?

Since then, have you been able to use any of the top ten suggestions to help you survive from day to day?

The importance of communication

Communication is the lifeblood of all relationships. It's a vital skill.

There are many blocks to good communication, such as anger, lies, emotional hurt, differences of opinion, legal stress, financial worries, addictions, and fear, etc.

Improving communication empowers us and will build our confidence in every area of our life.

We cannot change the way our ex communicates, but we have choices about how we want to communicate, and those choices will affect our recovery.

How to communicate well

1. Identify your historical patterns of communication. You will have built up habits in the way you communicate between you, some of which are healthy and some unhealthy.

Once a separation has started, a helpful first step is to reset your ways of communicating by means of a period of non-communication.

It's like rebooting a computer to restart the system. You need to start afresh.

For parents who need to make arrangements with their ex concerning the children, keep the communication businesslike and at the minimum level.

Take time to understand what has gone wrong. What are the unhealthy patterns of communication? What works and what does not work?

This may be incredibly hard, but it will pay dividends in the future. Be positive in the way you explain it to your ex – the aim is to create a more productive method of communicating for the long-term. For those with children, this is essential.

2. Learn the difference between facts and feelings.
When we talk, we transmit both facts and feelings. When a relationship works well there is an easy mix of both.

Now that your relationship has changed you will need to adjust your communication with your ex to be more factual.

Find someone else you trust with whom you can share your feelings.

Decide:
- What are the facts or concerns that need to be communicated to your ex?
- What are the feelings that you need to deal with?

3. Set healthy boundaries

In the same way that the walls of a home provide us with a physical refuge, the boundaries we place around our relationships provide us with an emotional refuge.

Drawing a definite line between what is appropriate and what is not appropriate is called setting a boundary.

Examples:
"You may no longer ring me at the office unless there is an emergency."
"I will not speak with you if you scream and shout."
"I am not going to open emails received from you after 9pm."

You have to make it clear to the other person that the boundary is there.

It may not be popular, but is it reasonable for your emotional well-being?

If so, put the boundary in place and get support to cope with the reaction from your ex.

A boundary is not there to punish the other person but to protect you emotionally.

When you feel less vulnerable, you can relax the boundary.

Small-group exercise

Which of these skills would help you: identifying historical patterns of communication, distinguishing between facts and feelings, or setting healthy boundaries?

4. Being a good listener

"Seek first to understand, then to be understood" (Stephen Covey).

To be good communicators, we need to be good listeners, who:

Pay attention – don't do anything else.

Listen without talking about our own agenda and opinions.

Be aware of bad listening habits:
- interrupting;
- giving advice;
- going off at a tangent;
- referring it back to ourselves (e.g. "Oh, I remember when that happened to me…");
- intellectualizing (e.g. "Psychologists have said that's not true…").

Reflect back – repeat the words back to the person to show them we've been listening and give them a chance to say something more.

Ask: "What's the most important thing you have said?" "Is there anything you would like to do about it?"

Exercise: Reflective listening in pairs

Take it in turns to be the listener and the speaker. The listener should reflect back and then ask:
- *What was the most important thing in what you've said?*
- *Is there anything you'd like to do about it?*

Group exercise

What did it feel like to be listened to?

Conflict resolution

Even if we get our communication right there will still be conflict.

Two dangers:
- never disagreeing;
- arguing, but never resolving the issues.

Conflict resolution is about understanding each other's concerns about something and finding a compromise that suits both people.

It is not about winning or losing.

There are some tools and skills that can really help in times of conflict.

Some problems may need the assistance of outsiders or professional experts.

Practical steps:

1. Commit to a positive attitude
Choose to approach the conflict with a good attitude.

Two unhealthy reactions: reacting aggressively or running away.

2. What is the issue?
If there are many issues, prioritize them.

Talk them through with a friend to help you work out what's most important to you.

Think creatively about possible solutions.

3. Find the best time, place, and method
What is the best time, place, and method for you to communicate?

A neutral venue is often helpful.

4. Confront the issue rather than each other

Avoid saying "You always…" or "You never…"

Avoid becoming personal or speaking negatively about them.

Keep your communication factual, and not feelings-driven.

Stick to points specifically related to the dispute you are resolving.

5. Seek outside inspiration

If necessary, bring in a neutral outsider: a friend, mediator, or counsellor.

Stop the negative spiral of unresolved conflict.

Small-group exercise

What would help you in dealing with your ex?

What did Kathy do differently this time in the role play?

We cannot change others, but we can take responsibility for the way *we* communicate.

Learning to be a good communicator is empowering and will build our self-confidence in all areas of life.

Session 3

Letting go

Small-group exercise

What did you find helpful from the last session?

Have you had any practical experience of any of the communication problems we covered?

No matter how good our communication is, it will not stop the pain of what has happened.

The key tool for letting go of the pain is forgiveness.

Forgiveness

Forgiveness stops us from being tied to the past and gives us hope for the future.

It breaks the chains that keep us emotionally bound.

It helps us to make the right choices free from the effect of past hurts.

It therefore gives us new life and freedom.

Forgiveness is one of the most misunderstood concepts.

We all carry within us ingrained ideas of what forgiveness means.

Why forgive?

1. Revenge does not work

We have an instinctive desire for justice and sometimes we want to bring about that justice ourselves.

If we start on this path it can quickly go out of control.

Vengeful acts can never compensate for the harm that has been caused.

2. If we do not forgive, we lose out

Lack of forgiveness affects every area of our life.

It's like carrying heavy baggage everywhere with us.

Our feelings of anger and longing for retribution do not hurt the person they're directed at. It's like drinking poison and hoping that the other person will die.

Archbishop Desmond Tutu said, "To forgive is not just to help others. It is the best form of self-interest."

When parents act as role models in showing forgiveness, their children are more likely to choose to forgive.

Small-group exercise

What do you think about forgiveness?

Forgiveness is NOT:

- condoning wrong behaviour;
- denying justice;
- denying that the hurt happened;
- demanding an apology;
- pretending that the issue does not matter;
- demanding that the person change;
- opening ourselves up to being hurt again – appropriate boundaries may be necessary;
- weakness – forgiveness takes courage.

Forgiveness means:

- releasing a person from punishment;
- ceasing to hold it against someone.

If someone does something wrong, we mark it down on an imaginary scorecard.

Forgiveness means wiping the slate clean.

Forgiveness is also needed for ourselves – for the things we have done wrong.

The marks against us can also be wiped clean.

Forgiveness has to be **chosen** – it doesn't just happen. Don't ask, "Can I forgive?" but instead, "When will I be able to forgive?"

We may need to forgive other people, as well as our ex, who have had an impact on our relationship, either recently or a long time ago.

How to forgive:

1. Recognize the hurt
This includes acceptance.

2. Acknowledge your responsibility, however small

Relationships are rarely "black and white"; it is unusual for there to be only one person completely at fault.

Apologize where you can.

"Sorry" acts like the handle on the door of forgiveness – it enables the door to be opened and the barrier to be removed.

3. Choose to release. There are two elements to this:

Choose to release a person from punishment.

Choose to cease holding it against them.

4. Make it an ongoing choice… again and again

Summary

We eventually arrive at a situation of **complete forgiveness**. We want the best for the other person.

Don't worry if you can't imagine complete forgiveness at the moment, but hold on to it as the ultimate goal of complete freedom for you.

If we do not forgive, we lose twice: once for the act against us, and second for holding onto hatred and pain.

Forgiveness is costly – we sacrifice our pride, our self-pity, and our need for justice, but we come out with something much greater: our freedom.

Things that hold back forgiveness:

1. Intense emotions

Allow them to subside first.

2. Enjoying the feelings of sympathy

Being the "victim" can make us feel that our lack of forgiveness is justified.

This can anchor us in the past.

3. Wanting to maintain power over your ex

You may think that holding it against your ex will help you.

In fact, it will prolong a language of winning and losing, which will make it harder to find a mutually acceptable solution and delay your recovery.

4. An insurance policy for the future

Focusing on the past will mean only that you are still affected by it.

5. It was so long ago

Events from a long time ago can still have an effect.

Small-group exercise

What is the most important thing for you on the subject of forgiveness?

Conclusion

Forgiveness enables you to let go. This is the single most important key to moving on successfully.

Session 4

Managing other relationships

Small-group exercise

What did you find helpful from the last session?

What are your thoughts about forgiveness?

Relationship breakdown not only affects our relationship with our ex, it also changes other relationships.

Friends

Every friendship will be affected by the breakdown.

Some friends may become closer, some may be awkward for a time, and others will be lost.

These changes can be painful and frustrating, but are very normal.

A few may emerge as trusted friends – nurture these.

Sharing friends with your ex can work as long as you have appropriate boundaries in place.

Don't ask your friends about your ex.

Some friends may hurt you – you may have to be willing to let them go and forgive them too.

Your social life may change.

This can be a time when new friendships form.

Consider taking up new hobbies to help make new friends and build your self-confidence.

Work

Try not to take the chaos of the breakdown into your workplace; keep it as free of the stress from this as possible.

If you feel your performance is being affected, tell your manager.

Parents and siblings

Our relationship with our parents will change.

We may need to ask them to limit what they say to us about their emotional response to the relationship breakdown, and limit what we say to them.

If our parents and siblings become too hostile towards our ex, it may fuel our own anger and bitterness, and harm our children.

In-laws

If you have children, your in-laws are your children's grandparents, uncles, aunts, etc. Try to maintain these relationships.

Speak to your in-laws only about your children and not about your ex.

These relationships can be very important for your children.

Small-group exercise

How are you managing your other relationships?

Children: The parent's perspective

Separation from children

One of the hardest consequences of separation or divorce is being separated from our children.

Be willing to acknowledge the pain, and to grieve for the loss of what could have been.

If you are unable to see your children regularly:

- Do all you can to make contact arrangements that are best for the children.
- Try to live somewhere close to the children if you move out of the family home.
- Stay in touch by email, letters, and phone or, if they are older, social media.
- Remember important events in your children's lives.
- Strive to speak respectfully of the other parent.

However hard and painful it is, keep letting go, give yourself space and time to recover, and make sure you have some close friends alongside to support you.

Some practical thoughts on parenting after separation:

Recognize that everyone makes mistakes as a parent – don't be overcome with guilt.

You are balancing your own personal survival with trying to be a good parent.

Recognize your emotional triggers and get support for yourself.

Times of collection of children can be very hard. Have a friend you can speak to if you think you'll get upset.

Release your children to enjoy their time with their other parent.

Have a regular meeting with your ex to discuss arrangements regarding your children. Keep it businesslike and run through any potentially difficult aspects with a friend beforehand.

Never cross-examine your children after a visit.

Find ways to help them open up and express their feelings.

Learn to handle shocking news appropriately in front of your children. Offload your feelings to a friend, not to your child.

Understanding the children's perspective

Regardless of our part in the breakdown of our marriage, our children never asked for this to happen.

Children want:
- to be "normal" – at school, with their peers, with their parents, with others;
- to be kept right out of the conflict between their parents;
- to be able to express what they are feeling – some children's suggestions are: to talk to a friend, a pet or someone neutral/to write a diary/to cry.

How we can help our children?
- Give them opportunities to express their thoughts and feelings.

- Recognize signs of anger – acknowledge them, help the child to work out what is the cause of the anger, and allow the child to let it out constructively.
- Model forgiveness so that they might see and choose to forgive those who have hurt them. We cannot expect a child to forgive if they do not see us doing it.

Shared parenting

Research shows that children from separated families benefit from shared parenting.

Choose to rebuild a "shared parenting" relationship with the other parent. In the early stages of separation, this may be only a goal for the future, but, as recovery comes, try to make it happen.

The goal is to shift from being parents who live together to being separate adults who share the parenting role successfully.

Consider sending a letter to the other parent, setting out various goals and guidelines for the way forward as parents. The "Parenting Together" letter (available on the Restored Lives website, www.restoredlives.org) suggests the following ideas:

Dear_____,

I am writing about our children. Whatever our thoughts are about each other, our children have never asked for this to happen. My hope is that we can put aside our issues and still be good parents to them, even though we will live apart.

The question for us is how do we shift from being parents who live together, to being separate adults who share the parenting role successfully? To start this process I have put down my thoughts below, but I would welcome your comments or additional ideas so that we can agree on the way that we share our parenting roles for the benefit of the children.

1. It would be good if we could tell them together that we are separating. We can tell them that this is not their fault, that we both love them, and that they will be spending lots of time with both of us.

2. Let's commit to be respectful about each other in front of the children. I recognize that they love you and the best thing for them is for me not to make unkind comments about you to them. I will find opportunities to talk about you in a positive way with them. Let's try to stop others, like our parents or friends, from being disrespectful about either of us in front of the children.

3. When we are in conflict about something, let's deal with it privately and not in front of the children.

4. At times of handover, let's be polite and friendly to each other, as these can be stressful moments for everyone.

5. When they are with me, I will not ask the children for information about you or your life, as it's not fair for them.

6. Let's make sure that we communicate directly with each other about their arrangements and their needs so that we never use them as the communication link between us.

7. Please can we try to agree similar house rules or boundaries together? We may not always agree, but at least then we can tell them that we've spoken about it, and that we know something's allowed in one of our homes and not the other. My hope is that they will experience us parenting together in this way, and will not be able to play us off against each other.

8. Can we try to attend some school events together, and sit next to each other at parents' evenings or school plays/matches, etc? I know that the children will appreciate this enormously if we can manage it in a polite way.

9. We will have a lot of arrangements to sort out, such as when they spend time with us both. It won't always be easy and we won't always agree, but I will commit to listen to you, and do my best to be constructive and polite in finding solutions to any disagreements. Let's agree to try to find solutions that work for both of us, rather than talking about winning and losing on every issue.

10. You share responsibility with me for our children and therefore, if any serious difficulties or challenges arise, I will discuss these issues with you rather than turn to others. Even though we have separate personal lives, I will make the effort to communicate with you about these issues straight away.

If we both follow this agreement, I believe that it will give our children a good hope for their future. I am confident that we can agree on the way forward for our parenting and will commit to putting all this into practice. I look forward to hearing your thoughts about how we can take this forward.

Small-group exercise

What would help you in parenting your children?

For people who don't have children:
What issues does this topic bring up for you?

Session 5

Legal matters

Small-group exercise

What did you find helpful from the last session?

Legal issues: Understanding the options

The most important tools to resolve legal issues are good communication, listening skills, and being able to resolve conflict, as covered in Session 2.

You are likely to need outside help to resolve the legal issues.

You have a choice of which process you will use to resolve the legal issues. Using a solicitor and a court process is **not** the only way.

This session aims to empower you to understand your options so that you can make the best choice for your family.

The goal is to have a fair outcome and also to have a relationship with your ex intact. This is especially important if you have children.

The choice of which process you use will have an effect on your recovery and on your relationship with your ex.

Options for resolving legal issues

| Working together to agree solutions | 1. Around a kitchen table
2. Discussions with a friend
3. Mediation
4. Collaborative law | Cheaper, quicker, empowering, builds relationships |

- -

| Working against each other – attack and defence | 5. Solicitors and court proceedings
(Barristers, court hearings, decision by judge) | Costly, takes longer, more stressful, destroys relationships |

Options

Around a kitchen table

If you still have good communications then you could sit round a table and agree a solution that is suitable for both of you.

During a relationship breakdown this may be impossible for many couples.

Discussions with a friend

If you have a wise and trusted friend then they may be able to sit with you both and help you to agree a solution.

Mediation

A mediator works with you, either in the same room or separate rooms, to resolve your legal issues and find your own solutions for the way forward.

It is a robust legal process that enables you to make your own decisions, helped if necessary with legal advice in the background.

If you have children, an important benefit is that your ongoing relationship as parents begins to be rebuilt as you discover you can still make decisions together.

Collaborative law

You each appoint a solicitor under a collaborative law agreement.

You all meet together around a table and your solicitor supports and advises you in your discussions to enable you to make your own decisions.

This process is more expensive than mediation, but is suitable when at least one person needs a legal advisor present in negotiations.

Solicitor and court proceedings

In this option you instruct a solicitor who represents you in court proceedings.

The court process is usually started immediately and a good solicitor will seek to negotiate a settlement on your behalf at an early stage.

A court process is where you and your solicitor defend your position against your ex. A solicitor is paid to defend your position in seeking the best outcome for you.

You are working **against** each other, which may cause increased conflict and hostility with your ex.

In the diagram, options above the dotted line leave you in control and making the decisions – **you are working together for solutions**.

These options are cheaper, quicker, empowering, and they build relationships.

The option below the line is more costly, takes longer, is more stressful, and can destroy relationships.

You can choose to create a constructive environment to address the legal issues.

The Family Justice Review in the UK found that the legal process is not about finding justice, but rather about finding the "least worst outcomes for families".

Which process is right for you? Where do you want to be on the diagram? What are the implications for your family?

Lord Wilson, President of Family Law Division said: "We still usually say to ourselves, 'I must find a solicitor'. But in many (though not all) cases, we would be better to say, 'We must find a mediator'."

Small-group exercise

What has been your experience of sorting out the legal issues? What was helpful, and what was not?

The legal issues to be resolved

Approach the legal issues with realistic expectations, especially if you feel like a "victim" in the breakdown.

The court process does not make any moral judgements; it looks at the practical consequences that arise when a relationship breaks down.

Maintain realistic expectations. The "no fault" system of divorce means that your ex will not be "punished" by the courts, even if you believe the breakdown is their fault.

In cases of abuse or violence then specific court processes are necessary.

Three specific issues to be resolved:

1. The legal ending of the marriage.

2. Arrangements for any children.

3. The finances.

These are each separate issues from a legal perspective.

Legal requirements in England and Wales

1. The legal ending of the marriage – the divorce
The legal requirement to obtain a divorce is that the marriage has "irretrievably broken down". This is proved by one of five facts.

Identify which fact applies to you and do it in the least acrimonious way possible.

2. Arrangements for any children
Parents are given "parental responsibility" and the children have "rights" (for example, the children have the right to enjoy a relationship with both parents).

Children need parents who can communicate together.

Avoid using lawyers or the courts to resolve disputes regarding the children, except as an absolute last resort.

Children suffer when there is parental conflict or hostility, as they usually want to please both parents. Court proceedings can cause them stress.

Use friends or professional mediators to help you reach any difficult decisions together as parents.

3. Resolving the finances

The UK does not prescribe a fifty/fifty split of assets. Instead, the courts seek to be flexible in dividing assets by considering a number of factors.

The exact outcome of any individual situation cannot be predicted.

Before any negotiations on finance can take place, you both need to give honest, comprehensive information about your financial situation on Form E.

This can be done in mediation or through lawyers depending which process you have chosen.

The financial disclosure provides the information needed to know what is in the family pot.

It may be helpful to ask a lawyer to advise you on what the upper and lower limits of the financial split would be if your case went to court.

Then you are ready to negotiate terms of settlement. The settlement will cover property, capital, pensions and maintenance for a spouse, and child support.

Wherever you are at with the process, always remember the end goal, which is to find a fair settlement so that you can both move on with your lives.

Using the Internet

For simple situations where there are no financial issues then this can be a good route to obtain a divorce.

If you have financial issues then be aware that an internet agreement made without separate legal advice might be vulnerable to be re-opened at a later date.

Civil partners or cohabiting couples

The different legal processes outlined in the first part of the session are the same for married couples, civil partners, or cohabiting couples.

The law for married couples and civil partners is the same. If you are a cohabiting couple, then the law on finance is very different and you need legal advice as each case would depend on your particular facts.

Conclusion

Try to remain focused on the main objective – to achieve a fair settlement and a restored relationship in the future.

More information is contained on the website: www.restoredlives.org.

Session 6

Being single and moving forward

Small-group exercise

What did you find helpful from the last session?

Tools for moving forward

The Restored Lives course is designed to give you hope and confidence to move forwards.

The practical tools are helpful not just for now, but also for many other situations that may occur in life.

1. Recognizing your feelings and thoughts

- Recognize and "own" your thoughts and feelings.
- Pain needs a response – it's no good leaving landmines buried and ready to explode.
- Think about the tools that will help you survive each day.
- Ban the thought "I am a failure".
- Seek to deal with longer-term problems such as anger, fear, and depression.

2. Building confidence through communication and resolving conflict

- A positive personal attitude – you can't change your ex but you can change your own attitude and the way you communicate.

- Being able to express yourself.
- Distinguishing between facts and feelings.
- Being a good listener.
- Creating healthy boundaries.
- Managing conflict in a controlled and constructive manner.

3. Letting go of the past

- Acceptance is important.
- Forgiveness:
  - **releasing the person from punishment;**
  - **ceasing to hold it against them.**
- Turning away from the past enables you to look ahead.
- Keeping on forgiving when memories haunt you.
- Finding freedom so you can let go.

4. Building successful relationships

- This is all about a changing environment.
- It's not unusual for your close friendships to change.
- Have a trusted friend alongside you.
- Look for new activities.

For children:

- Listen and respond to their thoughts and feelings.
- Rebuild a healthy shared parenting relationship.

The process of recovery doesn't happen in one quick step. Give yourself time, and make good choices along the way.

Seek continued help where you need it.

Take responsibility for building a new life.

Exercise

What does recovery look like for you?

Ongoing relationship with your ex

Some people may have a hope (however small) of re-establishing their marriage. If that is the case for you, beware of the divorce process getting out of control too quickly.

If you are not yet legally divorced, stop and think, "Is there anything more I can do to prevent it?" Make sure you will be able to look back and say you did all you could.

If both parties are willing – see a counsellor and/or do The Marriage Course (see www.relationshipcentral. org/marriage-course).

If only one party is trying to re-establish the marriage, then:

- Build up normal friendly relations.
- Get support.
- Affairs, addictions, or other inappropriate relationships need to stop.
- View any reconciliation as a new relationship.

"Wishing them well"

"Signing off" with your ex in a good way is an important step in moving on successfully.

Having sensible, polite, civil relations with your ex will put you in a far better position to move on.

If you can wish your ex well, it will help you obtain a sense of closure and not fear meeting them in the future.

For parents, this step enhances your ability to start a new shared parenting relationship.

Small group exercise

What are your hopes for the ongoing relationship with your ex?

Building strong foundations

Meaningful relationships are vital to us all.

These relationships can be with friends, family, children, at school, at work, with our neighbours, and even with our ex.

Beware of getting into intimate relationships.

We are more vulnerable now and a new intimate relationship is not the solution to our problems.

It can be difficult being celibate now that we are single:

- Channel sexual feelings into other activities.
- Close friends are a great compensation.
- Stay away from sexually explicit material.
- Find someone to whom you can be accountable.

Now is the time to build strong foundations for your future.

There are no lessons at school on how to make relationships work, but all our relationships can be strengthened by what we have learned on this course.

We need a willingness to keep learning so that we can build the foundations of strong, deep, fulfilling relationships across all areas of life.

Three key skills for doing this:

1. Understanding feelings and increasing self-awareness

Recognize thoughts, feelings, fears, beliefs, motivations, and emotions.

Self-awareness helps accelerate healthy change and develops better relationships.

Being self-aware helps you spot the emotional landmines.

2. Communication through expressing yourself and listening

Helps build relationships that will last.

Creates better understanding of the other person.

This is the lifeblood of relationships.

3. Conflict resolution and forgiveness

Be confident that you can successfully manage any conflict.

Do not be fearful of raising concerns.

Forgiveness is the last stage of conflict resolution.

Small-group exercise

What is your goal for the next few months?

Conclusion

Separation and divorce are a journey and we are all at different stages.

Through many ups and downs, we *can* achieve a recovery that leaves us stronger and wiser and offers hope for the future.

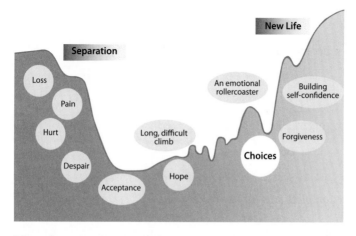

How do you want to move on?

Individual exercise

Consider the "Personal Statement":

I want to move on by...

I accept that...

I forgive...

Complete it as far as you feel able to.

Ultimately, there are no easy solutions to the problems that arise from separation or divorce.

Relationships can be challenging, but equally they can be the most fulfilling and satisfying part of life.

This course is designed to help you enjoy good, healthy relationships in every area of your life, and to rebuild a new life.

There *is* light at the end of the tunnel. A Restored Life is possible!

For more information, see our website:
www.restoredlives.org.